ST. PAT

to Elizabeth
with love,
Elsa

Elsa Corbluth *Photo: Iris Seymour*

St. Patrick's Night

ELSA CORBLUTH

PETERLOO POETS

First published in 1988
by Peterloo Poets
2 Kelly Gardens, Calstock, Cornwall PL18 9SA

ISBN 0 905291 92 1

Printed in Great Britain by
Latimer Trend & Company Ltd, Plymouth

ACKNOWLEDGEMENTS are due to the editors of the following journals and anthologies, in which some of these poems first appeared: *Sunday Telegraph Magazine*, *Other Branch Readings*, *Leamington*, *New Poetry 7 & 8* (Arts Council/P.E.N./Hutchinson, 1981 & 1982), *Outposts*, *Poetry Review*, *The Rialto*, *Sotheby's/Arvon Foundation Poetry Competition Anthology, 1982*, *Doors* (Word and Action, Dorset).

'The Jeweller's Shop' and 'Daffodils and Snowdrops' were read on *Poetry Now* (BBC Radio 3).

'Daffodils and Snowdrops' won 1st prize in the Bridport (South West Arts) Competition, 1981.

'Dirge for St. Patrick's Night' won joint 1st prize in the Cheltenham Festival Poetry Competition, 1981.

'Villanelle: I Live with Losers' won a runner-up prize in the Sothebys/Arvon International Poetry Competition, 1982.

WITH THE ASSISTANCE OF

SOUTH WEST ARTS

For Elín, my granddaughter, who lives in Iceland, and her parents, Adam and Hild.

Contents

page

Dirge For St. Patrick's Night

Rain on the red roses:
I had a daughter. I have none.
Grey fog on green hills rises:
I had two children. I have one.

Mist on the scented blossom:
she left, one afternoon,
face a flower, body lissom:
the same night burned to bone.

Needing to tend the needy,
so to find, and touch, Christ,
she reached his house unready
for this mocking of her trust.

Flowers of flame flourished redly
in her window while she slept:
love of dead Christ proved deadly,
her youth and my joy trapped.

Jesus said, suffer children,
not black-stick skeletons.
God's Joan or devil's cauldron?
Ash, all the holy ones.

At her grave's head, pale roses
picked with their claws of blood:
eighteen summers' slain praises:
under wet grass lies her God.

I use words: no-one listens.
I use tears with no ending.
My one girl the rain christens,
gutted house beyond mending.

Paper Girls

When my mother was a little girl
she cut out paper children
from her mother's sewing patterns,
piled up the pattern books in steps for a classroom,
and, bending the girls in the middle, she sat them
row upon row to give them a lesson:
she called them her paper girls.
If one was crumpled or the head was torn off
she was easy to replace with another paper cut-out.

When I was a little girl I was playing schools
with my row of dolls and my younger brother
when my brother accidentally knocked my favourite over,
smashed her head of German china, so I cried to crack the ceiling.
We took my girl, headless, to the doll's hospital.
They found her a head which was identical
except for the eyes. It had blue instead of brown,
but the same real hair and small mouth innocently parted.

My own little girl at the age of eighteen
gave away her dolls and went to London
to work in a hostel for homeless women.
She sat them round the table and gave them a party,
then went to bed with a smile like an angel.

One old girl in the early morning
lit a fire inside a cupboard:
nobody smelt or saw or heard it:
there were no alarms and no detectors.
The house flared up like a roll of cardboard
and with the house ten paper women,
one of them a girl, my pretty paper girl.

At the coroner's they couldn't find a face for her
with any kind of eyes, and her teeth were her signature.

They took her to church in a box of matchwood.
They dug her a hole in the heart of a village.
In the March wind rustled the paper mourners.
In my homeless house they ate their refreshments.

I took my snaps to the photographers:
they swelled them into paper daughters.
When people come I look in my cupboard
and bring them out and put them on the table,
my paper girls,
girls smiling in the garden,
smiling on horses, smiling with a boyfriend.
smiling in a boat, smiling on a mountain.

My paper girl had her name in the papers.
I didn't see how she was broken,
colour of eyes or hair or body.
I was only told she had a pure white soul,
my pretty little paper girl.

Shadows Of Grasses

Bending grasses
border the letter
she sent the Sisters
saying, "I have a burden
of love," saying, "Let Christ
guide me to you," saying,
between the grasses,
"I have had no rest:
I must give myself for my
replenishment."

Her "burden of love" is my burden
of loss. She burned. And the grasses
sprang in our garden,
shears and sickle
lying idle.
Sitting cloistered
under curtaining
grasses, listening
to speech of grasses,

I light with tears
the flowering grasses
that blow fair hair
against the ruffled
sea and uncertain
blue of the restless
sky. The Sisters wrote me:
"Think of the Mother Mary."

A forest of feathers
shadows the margins
of the poem I scratch on
this page's sunlit skin.

The waving wisps
that brush my lashes
and sketch lace on my paper
with her, in London, burned,
leaving behind
on this blond meadow
the charred shadows of grasses.

Photo: Elsa Corbluth

Last Night I Walked

Last night I walked with the contented dead
and introduced them each one to the other:
'Aunt Lily meet Miss Pugh'. I asked them whether
they'd met before. Each woman shook her head.
And the night after, turning in my bed,
I faced a face which had begun to wither:
waking, I knew it should be smooth instead,
although remembering the eyes were red,
eyes where the silences had come to gather.

The striped year stalks. The black bars of the night
and grey gaps of the day have not yet shown
the one face and the only eyes I crave
to pull back to my life as I pushed out,
with far less pain, that face into its own,
younger than all those dreams, in my womb's grave.

Out Of The Cold

(a bed-time story)

One Boxing Day, after all the fun and the goodies,
the film of the poor cold man lying dead in the snow,
his cold dog dying beside him, snow-weighted fir trees,
then plastic icicles and cotton wool snowballs
were suddenly menacing, as, under layers of blankets,
an eight-year-old girl lay sobbing for the cold man
and the still dog, hugging her soft-toy armfuls,
keeping her mother close to her repeating,
"That was in Canada where winters and woods are much colder.
Our snow is thin with hardly enough for a snowman.
You are warm and safe, so are your woolly animals."

She did not die of the snow or lie in a forest.
Ten years from then on her first night away from home
in a home for the homeless to keep people out of the cold
the same girl slept, secure in her kind intentions
to look after the poor cold people and keep them safely,
and, deep in the forest of bricks in the dead of the morning,
a black smoke blizzard, an avalanche of flame,
wiped out her peace and her pity, tore down the refuge
from the sharp March weather, tore up the poor warm people,

because all the dedicated, compassionate people
who thought of hot food and blankets and quotes from the Bible
and meant, we are here to see that you come to no harm
had never a notion of the greater danger of heat,
so the girl is as still as the snow in the dead of a forest
and half the poor people are frozen safe from their lives,

while on the screens of the people as safe as houses
comes a house as frail as a child's first pencil drawing
with the name of a child who trusted in her safety
and wanted to share it, believing in love that saves.

The Jeweller's Shop

So light, the miniature
gold crucifix
for a girl's throat,
lit on its fine gold chain
for her young neck,
sent in a velvet box
to mark her baptism.

Three months later
the cross is safe
in its box
and the girl is boxed
in a church's soil.

Six more months
and the mother walks
past the jeweller's shop
with its holy pendants.

How shall she mark
half a year's bereavement?

Behind the screen of rain
wear six long tears like baubles?

Gold, precious leaves:
lanes glitter girls,
the fields and buildings
run with girls.

The woman's fingers
comb the invisible
curls of yellow flame,
she carries on her shoulders
the fragile dry-wood frame
undressed of skin and gender.

The woman's walking quickens.
Her feet will be returning
each new glittering morning
in newly flaring loss
to the foot of a small gold cross.

Daffodils And Snowdrops

Hands exploding open
as though to mime a wall,
suns in my window's sky
that one day earlier
were chrysalis-tight;
and snowdrops, a cupful:
the quiet ritual
of taking from a drawer,
where it has lain
coffined for a year,
my daughter's photograph,
of standing it between
snowdrops and daffodils
to smile into the room.

Two days, nun-like,
I have spent facing
her yellow rush of hair
and her white laughter:
her denim buttonhole
sports a small daisy;
over her shoulder
is frothing yarrow;
above her summer head
hangs an apple-flower
her face's colour.

No fear of tears
buried her face from me
this year of winter:
these I accept like breath:
nor was it fear of anger:
this walks in all my steps.
It was the yarrow's snow
and the frost daisy,
stone wings of daffodils,
ice-drips of snowdrops,
and the white moon's
mask of sunlight.

Photo: Elsa Corbluth

"Pray For Us As We Pray For You"

The charity blankets, according to the fireman,
fell apart at the touch. He didn't describe the old women
or the girl of eighteen just arriving to minister to them.

He said nothing about the screaming
or whether he saw a flock of London pigeons
who were really angels for ten corpses coming,

conducting them to heaven
out of the house's scarlet halo, swimming
into the smoke, like craneflies, only thinner.

Sea winds cool her green bed. No second cremation.
No blaze of flowers. We had a Mission collection
to give us a grain of sense in the idiot ocean
we stoned with questions.

The Mission even mislaid some of the money.
The fireman told how with simple fire precautions
none of this need have happened.

You little hooded women,
you grow your god like mildew on the bread
you offer to the drowning.

You claim this was divinity-intended.
You chant at dawn to your vague lord who's running
our earth like your accounts, the fire beginning
in the next room. Go out and do your slumming
where there is nothing human.

If there were gods, then your twittering vision
who takes a drunken vagrant prone to arson
for his handmaiden
would be extreme blaspheming.

Only Christ is supposed to forgive sins:
so you won't expect to be pardoned
by the mortal parents
of the child you let light to a legend.

You have left us no more blood
for the making of future children.

Even if God
itself came out one Sunday,
spreading itself like hoarfrost over the playing
fields, I would not be praying
for you, me, anyone.

Sonnet: What Was My Game?

I played survivors in my dead girl's room
and dressed my middle age in her young shirt,
took out her treasured toys (salvaged, for whom?)
like pressing nettles to fend off their hurt.
When bluebells grew like tears there was nowhere
to run, no woods, no hills, not any tree
to give one leaf which I would find so rare
that for one blink of time I could be free
of the ground's hollow and the vacant sky.
Mature transvestite: was my game a sin
(when cliff-tip, wave-haul, would be less a lie)
to act inhabiting the youthful skin

my child does not, and not to know my place—
to share the new room for her burnt-off face?

Buttermere

Cocked on the fell, a little party hat,
with toy steps to the door,
the church I chose to enter.
There in the kind and confined dark I sat
and wept for my burned daughter.

Out, full moon in the trees and the road jaunty
running about the fells,
clatter of churns like bells
ringing me to the farm at the valley centre,
the rough skin of its walls,

the bulging ceiling where we laughed to sleep
and laughed awake to light
of butter and June heat,
cupped safely in these hills that rain will steep
soon, they are too clear-bright.

Photo: Elsa Corbluth

Early into the church again, fell-shod,
over the dazzling grass
I went to my first mass,
six of us there together. The priest stood
in his appointed place,

saying, as I came late, "Pray, in this week
of violence . . ." (Pope shot,
the woman-ripper caught).
A spring ago the daughter I still seek
laughed goodnight, and was not.

And for that stripped stretched man up there she died.
Letting no sparrow fall
he left no girl at all
but bits of bone black as the dark church side.
I have not come to call

From its white grave two thousand years of dust
or from the aching space
beside me her non-face,
but to commune with her in me, and just
these five, live in her place.

One is a fair-haired girl, the rest old women.
I follow what they do,
taking in my hands too
the disc that looks like honesty in autumn,
tastes like a papery new

icecream cone, and the vicar says "Be thankful".
Is this her firm young body,
and is this bloody
drip of wine her dead red life, a dam full,
and am I anybody?

As we go out he takes off his grave-clothes
and his grave expression,
asking me no question.
I lift my rucksack. "Hallo"; his smile soothes
the edges of my mission.

"Hallo" I answer, turn to face the mountains:
every groove and gully,
spine and shoulder fully
focused, in the clean lens of the morning.
I walk out of the valley,

up to the ridge where once she rode inside me,
and, after, on my back,
then toiled, a child. The track
still leads to where she strode as though to guide me,
a strong girl; and the lack

of all those she became and all those others
she will not be, I take
on to my back, and break
another barrier, descend, as rainlight gathers,
into a further valley for her sake.

Photo: Elsa Corbluth

Ysabeau—Her Lament

On 30th May 1431 a girl of 19, Jeanne d'Arc, from the village of Domremy, Lorraine in France was burnt at the stake for heresy and witchcraft. In November 1455 her mother Ysabeau was among those presenting evidence to clear Jeanne's character posthumously and reinstate her.

On 18th March 1980 a girl of 18 from a village in Dorset, England, died in a fire (in the absence of fire precautions) at a hostel for homeless women run by nuns in Kilburn, London, where she had gone to work as a voluntary helper twelve hours before. Nine homeless women also died.

This girl, like Jeanne, believed that God had called her to this mission. Both girls died, in effect, at the hands of the religious bodies for which they had fought or worked.

Jeanne, Jeanne,
you would have left us for your man,
and there was one,
shy, with a soft beard,
to be added to our sons.
His mother had no daughters.
We were ready to have shared
you, Jeanne. We already shared you
with the Lord God, the ghost Jesus, his hooded mother
and three neighbourhood saints.
They stood, tall trees, at the top of our tangled garden.

Another girl your age has a young son
and other maids have nothing to do but look pretty,
it depends on their station.

Oh Jeanne,
your wide hips should have carried children,
your full breasts filled them with your own health.
People warmed themselves in the light of your face.
It is dark now. You are nowhere any more.
Your red dress is hanging on your door.

We must all be delivered from life as surely
as a mother must be delivered of her baby,
but as there is premature birth
there is also premature dying.
Jeanne's mother has only
stones on a river bed,
beads for a rosary,
and all Jeanne's voices are still. The saints are silent,
God in his wisdom has gone underground and the buttercups
are innocent of knowledge,
the cuckoo, ignorant, chuckles.

In the village
some avoid me, some look down or sideways,
talking of crops and rains, of their sons and mine.
If we should face each other
in my red eyes they see a burning girl
no tears will cool.

I sweep. I bake.
All day the busy neighbours
enter my cool stone house and bring me presents
of flowers, prayers, tears and their hands' hopeless gestures,
saying "Words cannot express", but words have to.
I cannot cry with them. My crying is rooted
and racks me to the womb when I am alone.
My eyes are heads of pins,
inside my scalp I wear a stinging brain.
It is two years since blood·blotted my legs;
I can have no more daughters.

Jeanne, oh Jeanne,
never came June so green,
never lay long grasses
so sleek, the tails of squirrels,
quills, silver flowers of frost
and the gilt fleur-de-lis
all leaning to me as I bow and weep,
continuing the stitching Jeanne began.

Good people, do not speak to me of Death.
This is not Death. It is a dead girl,
not even a lifeless girl, but something raked
out from a finished furnace,
something that has no face.

Do not speak to me of risen life like the preacher.
If a piece of meat
drops from the spit
into the fire's centre
it will not rise as sheep
to suckle its lambs, grow wool and be patient in winter.

I have seen only the smallest of burns,
a blotch, a blister.
I had seen only one dead, apart from the animals,
one yellow old woman
going out of her life in her sleep.
We were waiting for it to happen.
Then they tied her chin to the top of her head
with a cloth like a wimple.

Then your small sister
who was always fragile
fell cold as a lily one Christmas.
Most families have one
the Lord takes for his own.
We are taught to accept one cross
and she was a sweet light one for us to wear.
I strewed marguerites on her little grave mound,
looked up and smiled to see my neighbours
on similar errands.
I had three sons. I was strong,
and I had you, Jeanne.

But Jeanne, my young woman,
they threw her heart in the Seine
and nothing remains.

Oh my Jeanne,
there was no time to sit down and explain
before you were gone.
I would have said, it is not your war,
you are wanted here:
sampler, not banner,
not sword but spindle,
brown arms and not cold armour.

You were always a bold rider,
straddling our plough horse like a boy,
your strong knees guiding him home,
in your maid's skirt, brazen.
When I hear the beat of riders
my heart will stop.

Guarded by randy soldiers in your prison
you dressed as a soldier to remain a maid.
This was your greatest trespass:
if you had been a soldiers' wench,
flaunting your red skirt to the coarse red faces,
there would have been no burning.

The poppies flare and char in the sun;
out of my hedges
poke the curved branches
of pink wild roses,
little girls' lifted faces,
a crown for little Jeanne,
a crown of needles
for her mother's eyelids.

There are the rumours, Jeanne,
that you did not burn,
that you will lift our latch in dark of winter
and come to our fireside.

I close my eyes and see the ashen armour,
a sexless rider heading for my meadows
to bring me tidings.

In the market place,
the clearing in between the peering houses,
space thickening with spectators,
high as her Son of man, and woman,
hammered to his red heaven,
in the dry market
she sold herself to her Lord,
and the Lord grimaced at her, saying,
It is the price we pay
for such high-mindedness.

The sun is strong. It dries up my wet face.

The audience has taken its tears home.

My door was open to the setting sun.
St. Margaret, St. Catherine
came in with a heavenly grin.
St. Margaret said, "I have come from Rouen.
You have a beautiful daughter."
"But I have no daughter."
"She is with Christ," she replied,
"You are a lucky mother."
St. Catherine, in her habit, bent her head.
held out a sprig to me;
I smelt it, rosemary,
but I saw her as a gypsy crone
peddling her charms of lucky common heather.
St. Michael, busy that day from an archangel's enthronement,
sent a representative,
young, curly-haired:
"You are beautiful" he said, with the brogue of a different region
(my apron was full of cowslips, bluebells, wood-anemones
for Jeanne's memory.)
The Blessed Virgin herself sent our house a personal message
and would have been there but for blessing the dying
in a distant eastern country.
How I ought to have felt honoured!

Jeanne, Jeanne, Jeanne,
your friends don't believe in your sin,
and I don't believe you a saint,
but they say that you must be one
or the other. I know you were good, our Jeanne.
They say they remember
my girl wading into the river,
white clothes of her modesty, sails,
her face alight and holy,
a moon on the water,
"Like a bride" they said, "going to her beloved.
She married the Lord that day."
From the chapel-dim woods the children
gathered flowers and leaves for garlands
to decorate Our Lady of Domremy—
a country custom.

The Lord Inquisitor
called this an evil practice.

If she was not wicked, then she must be exalted.

Jhennette,
your room is a child's.
There are little toys among
the texts you could not read
but were taught to repeat.
Ask the fire that took your girlhood
if you, the Maid, were virgin.
I say, it does not matter.

They say, your little Jeanne was pure as water,
as if the gross earth had not touched her feet.
If she had left a baby for my cot
instead of wooden crosses on her wall
anyone could have had her sky-blue winding sheet.

A peasant doll, one child inside another,
inside another, inside all her mothers,
all are charcoal.
My past and all my futures
are in this charred and brittle box,
spirit burnt out.
Your spirit is not on the smoking sky
or in the earth's foundations.
Your spirit suffocated.
Without your limbs' dress
and without your face
Jeanne has no spirit, nor have I Jeanne's spirit.

Grasshoppers, whispering loudly of warmth, are living,
flies and beetles dance their little spirits,
butterflies ask, prove, nothing in their floating.
Soft air, its touch unbearable, is pleasure
that Jeanne cannot, and will not, ever feel,
nor all Jeanne's generations after me
who died before conception.

There is no flowering like a daughter's children.
We love our sons with a difference,
not less or more, but their sons are another woman's.
A daughter's rich soft hair and her smooth forehead
return her mother's youth.

Jeanne should have buried me with a small weeping,
not herself melted to offal, to an offering
to the unconsecrated river.

They held her to the crowd, a blackened spectre,
recognisable only by her teeth.
In Domremy we knew her by her smile.

Where are your breasts, Jeanne,
your babies nuzzling ashes?
Where are your years and years?
What boneless charger will you ride in heaven?

Sometimes a summer storm darkens our house.
Sometimes with Jacques, my husband,
we lash out at each other.
I say "You let her go—where were your man's hands?"
He says "You were willing—where was your woman's entreaty?"
There is thunder between us.
Uselessly, I long for us and all her brothers
to have tied her, chained her in the cell of her room,
and told the saints to visit another girl,
and, in that other, to be mistaken for demons,
so, when the other had burned,
we could have said to her, Jeanne,
we, who gave you your life, have kept it for you again.

One night I dreamed of Jeanne
splashing delightedly in a small puddle
at my house door,
a girl of three or four,
when suddenly the puddle
deepened. Rapidly she sank
right out of sight. Quickly I seized her clothing
and pulled with a great effort.
I got her out, her heavy living body,
to wake, in flooding disappointment.

The next night I dreamed I had taken
Jeanne to a strange house.
She was about sixteen,
thick waving hair and glowing skin.
I took her to a room. Looking back in
I saw her sleeping, perfect.
I then opened another door:
that room was empty
but for a broad stone step.
I awoke, shaking.

Brave Jeanne,
you took your chance in battle like a man
and your chance won.
A man might have come home.

It is not clear which lord
gave, or took, the sacrifice of Jeanne,
Inquisitor or Lord of all creation.
Neither will come to Lorraine
to my meat knife:
if I stop any life
it will have to be my own.

They say there is not time:
grain, linen and broom
will take your mind off, woman.
I grind, stitch and disturb.
I am penned
in a house of men.

In years to come I, Ysabeau,
with my white seed head and crooked back
will give my testimony,
shaken and weary, drizzling my thinned tears,
pleading, at last, for Jeanne's enshrinement
in time for my entombment.

What shall I do with all my years,
girls singing past me, beech leaves in their hair?
Where shall I hide at weddings?

They tell me, Jeanne, if you had stayed at home
no-one would have heard your name;
they tell me I have yielded up my child
to Christ and history.
Instead of grandchildren will spring
stone crosses to our woods
and shining girls of bronze and hollow maidens
on iron horses
across her motherland,
over the discovered world,

while Ysabeau still longs in every finger
to touch the eyebrows, cheeks and hair
of Jeanne, human,
and heaven only sends
angels with their feet of air,
their fine mist hands
and a dead saint's candle.

Fog

I like fog,
hills rubbed out,
tomorrow, the next hour
even, scrubbed.

My life is
half a flat field,
two wet trees.

The unleafed
trees are lungs;
heart is a blind
continuation
of walking feet.

The eyes of cars
search only
three cats' eyes
distance.

Gulls are grounded,
then rise, pretending
to be swans
(the sea a legend).

This fog is
pearl.
Fogs I recall
were sandy,
palpable;

and I was
carried
safely
through an unbelievable
exciting element.

Once I swung
a long-clothes
baby doll
upsidedown
by her pretty
gown, tired of
carrying her.

Carry, carry,
carrying:
put it down;
no-one can see:
it is too foggy.

Want it,
mine,
I want it:
it's a girl,
sleeps all night,
sleeps all day,
good baby.

Ah, to be free
of all those
equally clear,
equally impossible
choices,

to be carried
inch by inch
wound
in a woolly mist,

and these words
sent to glory:
glory? is only a
thicker
fog?

God Calls In Chester Cathedral

In the morning the guided walk with the American tourists ended
here.
Led by an ex-military gentleman with crisp voice and a crisper collar
(after King Charles's tower on the Wall, the Roman central heating,
medieval bridge, canoes in rapids, Tudor housefronts
and all that old-rose stone) we came by the Visitors' Entrance
into the shade of this soaring pink stone forest, quiet
except for the ring of a few shoes on the tomb-floors.
The intricate carving on the little turrets above the choir-stalls
and vivid mythical beasts on the undersides of the seats
seemed to me wonders only men could have created,
and no god, blundering down the aisles, formless, in amazement,
to marvel at the miracle of stained glass, old and muted or new
primary blue,
could put up such a structure in the celebration of itself.

In the afternoon, at the museum of Roman lettered stones
and exhibition of pre-neon shops, unpackaged grain and sawdust
bar,
I kept meeting a foreign lady from the tourist party
who told me there would be a concert at six-thirty in the Cathedral.
I said I would go to it. There was a language difficulty.
It was, of course, a service on a Sunday evening. Evensong.
I still went. I am not, however, a churchgoer;
I do not have a hat or stockings or shoes of that kind.
No, but I had an evening to spend in Chester.
The theatre was closed. It was Kung Fu at the Odeon.
I wasn't hungry, it was too early for the Bed and Breakfast
and the river looked too cold and grey, wind getting up
and the boats moored, so I went in, sat at the back. I didn't kneel.

The ornamental choir seats were not used, only the new plain wood.
There were some pretty girls in the choir. They were too far off
for me to hear their words distinctly, though the space resounded
with the organ, like the sea's shout in a cave.
There was, in the trembling of candles and swinging of cassocks,
chanting of choir, muttering of congregation,
a quietening absence of conflict, as in a forest,

an overarching acceptance, a parental hand on the head
and no being expected to smile. The words ran their course.
The sermon was on Matthew and his call to God:
"When God called Matthew he left everything and went. When God calls you
you must answer the call". When we had paid our money
and got our blessing, a beautiful nun like a saint
touched me on the arm and asked, "Are you a visitor?
Will you come and have a cup of tea with the Canon?"
She gathered up people with such a cool warmth
and immaculate smile that I thought of the Canon
with his door open and the cups waiting and no-one coming
and of myself, the evening early and cool, and nowhere to go, so I followed.

In that historical house the Canon's angel
administered tea while the Canon himself moved among us
speaking to each one in turn. He didn't stay long
with the draggle-bearded man and his dirty rucksack,
but mouthed to the sleek youth with a simpering mother,
"I wish they'd *wash*". I made some conversation
with the rag-beard, asked if he'd come from far and he said "Chester".
The rest of us *had* washed, some, perhaps, in blood. I took up
the prim tone of the rest, told where I came from, said I liked Chester,
gave a clue that I was on a literary visit.
The Canon enthused, with a cultivated laugh, on P. G. Wodehouse,
quoting, "The genteel moon ..." A little imp alighted on my shoulder.
I mentioned R. S. Thomas, "also a clergyman", recommending his poem, 'The Minister'.
"Read what he says about *his* moon; I won't tell you",
(in my head quoting: "You did not see
The moon's bum rubbing the window pane").

The little imp then tapped my neck, so, at an impulse,
as the Canon was about to move on to the next Sunday lady,
I said, "I am tempted to ask you something more serious".
He switched off his benign smile, gave me his full attention,

motioned to a fussy little lady to refill her own teacup.
Suddenly it was combat. Better than Kung Fu. I reminded him
of the sermon
and the call to God. "My daughter thought God called her.
She went to work for the homeless. The home was burned
by one of the homeless. My daughter was eighteen,
on the top floor. It was her first night there.

There were no fire alarms. I have no daughter.
The nuns said she was needed by God. What was this God
that called her to God's work and then prevented it?"

The Canon, kindly, used the usual clichés. I forget them,
except the one about ideals: "She died with her ideals intact".
(I thought of Lorca's Bernarda: "My daughter died a virgin").
I was sorry for him, cornered, so I pulled my punches,
said only, "I have shopped around, in tiny churches and in cathedrals,
but haven't met this God, this "good" in what happened.
Life is good. God is life. Death is for the old, tired, finished,
not for eighteen. Not for Christ at thirty".
I let him shake my hand and close the conversation:
"Thank you for telling me".

                                        And still I tell it.
Walking across the cobbles, breathing the green evening,
God, I had *my* conviction. How many years of study
does it take to make a Canon, dress in God's black fabric?
deal words like Christmas games and dispense tea
in flowery cups?

                          Pray God, does God
burn young girls as they sleep with their ideals
unbroken, nail young men, awake, to crosses?
If so, how many million Jews, scorched Japanese,
how many African children.

                                        does God need for his breakfast?

Roses At Myvatn

(Iceland)

And in that steaming landscape
of ash and grit, hot powder,
the mountains smeared with colours
that follow fires, blue-greys and orange-ochres,

where fissured rock breathes sulphur
and where, in blood-warm water
whose veins run deep in parted
valley floors, the naked campers wallow,

rounding the dust-road's corner,
close to the lake's blue shiver
and those stark fire-blown arches,
travellers are proudly shown the rare rose garden:

"This year the roses budded
but none of them will open.
Not every year they flower:
sharp winds, burnt soil, brief sunlight are not kind to roses".

And not this year and never
will that rose show her petals.
These buds are young dead daughters
against my life's cold lake and its black firescape.

My Future

My future lay asleep
And wrapped in wool
Where snow had wound to keep
The hollows full.

My future's face was new
And old as blood.
New snow had shivered through
And lit the wood.

My future sat awake
While winking leaves
Played on her arms to make
Her shadow sleeves.

When four I was afraid
Of women old
And veiled in black: I stayed,
In sunlight, cold.

My future gave that world
A different form:
Seas growled while she lay curled,
In darkness, warm.

My future dared the waves,
On branches swung,
Eased body out of caves,
A woman, young.

My future spilled her tears
For women old,
Abandoned to the years,
On springnights cold.

She took her future face
Into the past:
My future found no place
Where she could last.

My future self was scorched
To no return.
The past stood by and watched
My future burn.

(Old woman in a dress
As green as paint:
Old woman come to bless,
Blind as a saint.)

The future rain may spill
Or leaves may shake:
No trees, no morning will
My future wake.

So age my future wound
In a red sheet
And left her in the ground
At my life's feet.

Good women wind their spools
In their white veils:
Our futures were their fools
And our hopes, nails.

Two Sonnets For Two Islands

There are two islands I should not revisit
but keep as fresh as photographs of flowers.
Sark in the south, whose heather breath allows
no whiff of cars, lies dozing like a lizard,
three and a half miles skull to scaly tail,
rock-lidded tide-pools filled with sky, profound
and blank as crystal futures, tide-chased sand
and tide-blacked cliffs, the distance just a mile
across the green back to the far sea fall—
caverns of rainbow sea anemones,
the secret creature gardens of the seas.
The pools still mirror and the blind caves feel
    in the slow-changing island's bones and veins
    a family of four. But three remain.

The other island banished from my present
is northern Barra where her name was sung
out of the midnight boat, with everyone
chorusing on the quay. As we two listened,
(Gaelic, and speech of water) I said, "Give
her that name, if we ever have a girl."
The road that rings that island glitters shells
powdered to sun-dust. There, her name's alive
in others' children. On my own bare rock,
stranded without her, I must learn to scratch
from this a meagre living, turn and watch
the tide of stranger-children at my back.
    Her face, my grief, are fresh as island air.
    She'll leave those islands if I go back there.

Delicacy

Death is indelicate.
But should I give you
tasteful death?

Death, arranged in floating
Burne-Jones muslin,
a sweet breeze wafting,
a curl carefully straying
and the pale rosebud mouth
giving up its dainty ghost?

Shall Death, white warrior,
one neat incision
cleanly dispatching him
to the frost-feathered angels,
be borne at moonrise
to his noble triumph?

Must we poke noses
into the secret cell
where the self-starved youth
is discovered,
grey cadaver,
in his stench of decay?

Ought we to part the smoke
and open streaming eyes
to the fire's bloodlit blades
that cut flesh
like a nightdress
off the sleeping girl?

Our screens and newspapers give us our daily starvation,
our close encounters with the spindly, balloon-bellied, humanoid
shadows out of the saucer from another world.

Statistics show us figures of the dead and dying, charred
in distant Japan. Films simulate the black burn-bubbles
on actors' limbs and faces. Some of the stills are even genuine:
that is a real heat-blasted baby (would now have been middle-aged
woman or man.) That, too, is history's carnage.

And you can make it up, tell of a searing future,
compose a ritual graphic warning,
fashion a spell to make it go away.

You say, what you would tell us is too recent,
too close in place.
Time has not washed the wasted limbs
nor distance
buried the crackling bones,
prophecy dignified them.
Such haste to give expression is indecent.

I did not want to scorch you,
nor yet withhold the substance
that I might learn to bring you.
Nor did I choose my subject.

In my peacetime privilege,
western sufficiency,
I did not understand
starvation,
suffocation
in the bodies of my own, advantaged, children.

You, young in their time, tell me, can you?

Villanelle: I Live With Losers

I live with losers, losers understand
and speak a language I need not translate:
home in my landscape they defend my land;

for losers light their loss and keep it fanned:
a black house can't afford an empty grate:
I live with losers, losers understand.

Yet losers laugh when laughter comes to hand:
loss is not poker-faced in solemn state.
Home in my landscape they defend my land

where losers cry and crying is not banned,
for we are groundless and we have no weight.
I live with losers, losers understand.

No loser claims existence can be bland:
(snow bites, abrasive, and fire tears like hate)
home in my landscape they defend my land.

Loss grows no skin to graft over the brand
and holds no passport to a sweeter state.
I live with losers, losers understand:
home in my landscape they defend my land.

Elsa Corbluth was born at the London end of Kent. She spent the Second World War in Salisbury, Wiltshire, left school at 14, and lived in Kendal, then Westmorland. In her early 20's she married, lived in Nottingham, and had done some 35 or so different jobs (from library work to distributing free samples of pea soup, and many categories between) before having a son and a daughter and moving to Dorset where she has lived for the past 25 years, the last 3 separated, now divorced.

She has been writing verse since the age of 7 but did not publish until the age of 40. Since then her work has appeared in leading poetry magazines and anthologies and has been broadcast on *Poetry Now* (BBC Radio 3). She has won a number of national poetry prizes, including joint 1st prize in the Cheltenham Festival Poetry Competition, 1981, and 1st prize in the Bridport Arts Centre poetry competition in both 1979 and 1981.

As a mature student, she did a B.A. in Combined Creative Arts at Alsager, Cheshire, and an M.A. in Creative Writing at Lancaster University. She has published a few short stories and is working on a novel. *St. Patrick's Night,* Elsa Corbluth's first full collection of poetry, is an attempt to deal with the death—see back cover—of her daughter, Eilidh.

An *Outposts* pamphlet of poems by Elsa Corbluth's daughter Eilidh is still available. All proceeds go to Oxfam.
(*I Won't Paint Any Tears* by Eilidh Boadella, price £2.00 post free. Cheques payable to Oxfam, but orders to: Elsa Corbluth, Hawthorn Cottage, Rodden, Abbotsbury, Weymouth, Dorset DT3 4JE.)